The Story of Cosham

RON BROWN
in conjunction with
Wally Greer

"*Down Memory Lane I linger long,*
Till evening shadows fall.
To dream of golden days bygone,
And radiant hours recall."

AF471178

© Ron Brown 1983

All rights reserved. No part of this publication may be
reproduced without the prior permission of Milestone
Publications except for brief passages in criticism or review.

Phototypesetting by Inforum Ltd, Portsmouth
Printed in Great Britain by
Conifer Press, Fareham, Hampshire

Published by Milestone Publications
62 Murray Road, Horndean, Hants PO8 9JL

First impression 1983
Reprinted 1985

British Library Cataloguing in Publication Data

Brown, Ron, *1932–*
    Fairdays and tramdays : the story of Cosham.——
    2nd ed.——(Down memory lane; 7)
    1. Cosham (Hampshire)——Social life and customs
    I. Title   II. Series
    942.2'792   DA690.C74/

    ISBN 0–903852–43–8

It was a fine sunny day, and George was quite content to wait on the pavement of Cosham High Street, whilst his wife was engaged in the shop he had his back to, buying something or other for one of the grandchildren. To George's mind, it seemed that the members of his family celebrated birthdays every five minutes!

George was not very keen on shops when the weather was behaving itself, he preferred the fresh air. Well, as fresh as it can be in this polluted age that we live in, with cars and delivery vehicles rumbling by on their way up the High Street. He just stood there, gazing into space, oblivious of the activity around him, his mind was in another world, in a different age.

Suddenly, he felt a tap upon his shoulder. "Hello, George! My word, I haven't seen you for ages, how are you?" George turned to see who had broken into his thoughts of the past. "Well, I'll be blowed, hello Harry, it is nice to see you once again."

The two men warmly shook hands, and immediately launched into the verbal niceties relating to health, wealth, and their family fortunes. As may be expected when old friends meet after an interval of several years, the conversation turned to days long gone, when neither of them had thoughts of rheumatism and creaking joints, or of being engaged in the weekly trips to the post office to collect one's old-age pension!

"It is strange that I should meet you like this Harry, before you came along I was thinking about our old school. Cor, the times we walked up and down this High Street in procession, with Mr. Budgen up front leading the way, I can remember his face as clearly as I can see yours."

"Yes," said Harry, "It is the same with me. Mr. Budgen was a great chap, wasn't he? You know, I am afraid the High Street has changed a lot since those days, you would hardly recognise it now, apart from the odd landmark here and there. Do you remember Fanny Barber's sweet shop? It was near the school gates in the High Street, and some of the lads used to lead her a merry dance, asking for sweets from the top shelf, then whilst she had her back to them they would pinch sweets from the front trays!"

"Oh, yes, I can remember that also" chuckled George. "I don't know, things were so different then, Cosham was just a village surrounded by fields, and everybody seemed to know each other. It's all rush and tear nowadays, they cannot be bothered to even say good morning, folk are not half so friendly as they were in the old days."

"You know," continued George, "I feel sorry for the youngsters of today, they may have their coloured televisions and space invader machines, and have more money in their pockets than we ever had, but they are missing out on the simple pleasures. Cor, do you recall the marvellous times we had playing in the fields, the summer evenings seemed to remain light for so much longer in those days. And when the Portsdown Fair was on, Cosham really came to life, with thousands of people making the trek from Pompey to join in all the fun of the fair. Ah, happy days!"

"Yes, indeed" replied Harry. "The sad part of it is that when we have passed on, all our fond memories of the Cosham that has gone will be lost forever, and nobody really cares, even though they are part of the village's history. Ah well, that's life, it was nice to have met you again George." The two old friends shook hands, and went their different ways. The traffic continued to rumble up the High Street.

But all is not lost. For the sake of George and Harry, and countless others who have seen Cosham grow from a sleepy country village into the thickly populated Portsmouth suburb it is today, we will attempt in the following pages to provide a nostalgic glimpse of the Cosham of yesteryear.

Before commencing on this journey into the past, we would like to state that just as several brands of cigarettes have health

Looking down from the top of the High Street, note the fountain.

High Street. The shop on the corner of Southampton Road now shows a preference for bicycles instead of hardware.

warnings, this book also begins with a warning. It is not directed at the reader who prefers his history in the usual text-book style, nor does it pretend by any means to be the full history of Cosham, it is merely a gentle reminder of the village's quieter days, its characters, and some of the small businesses that served its residents.

Before we sally forth in search of darkest Cosham, it might be an idea to get the name of the village correct at the beginning. We do not wish to delve too deeply into the 'In Hertford, Hereford and Hampshire, Hurricanes hardly ever happen' routine, but it has come to our notice that a great number of people pronounce the name as 'Cosh-em'! It is in fact 'Cos', followed by 'ham'. Thank you Professor Higgins, now we can get on with the story.

When Knights Were Bold

Welcome to the year 1086, when knights were bold, and ladies were quite happy that they were! Of course, the Readers Digest was not around in those days, but if it had been it would no doubt have presented its "Book of the Year" award to the Domesday Book, the historical survey of that period. At the time of the Domesday survey it was recorded that the King held four hides of land at Cosham, which was then part of the Royal Manor of Wymering.

William de Cosham held land in Cosham worth 60 shillings by serjeanty, and it was his obligation to provide one armed man in time of war for the defence of Portchester Castle. If you are wondering what use a man with one arm would be in a battle, we must explain that he had two arms and his own weapons of war! Anyway, when William died his lands were taken over by his son, Peter de Cosham. Peter appeared to have several daughters, and when he passed on the two eldest divided the land between themselves. The eldest daughter was named Agnes, and her part

of Cosham passed on to her son, Peter, who in turn conveyed the land to Henry Wade in 1269. Henry's son, John, inherited it, and it was around this period that our game of Happy Families struck a sour note, for in 1288 John Wade went before the King in an attempt to regain land that had been taken into the King's hands for John's default against Margery, his father's widow. The matter appeared to get sorted out, and during the following three hundred years or so this part of Cosham was held by a succession of families that included names such as William de Erlee, John de Erlee, Thomas de Sandford, Laurence de Pageham, and John Wallop. By 1604 it was in the hands of the Brunings, who also held the Manor of Wymering, and from this time onwards Cosham evidently became merged in the Manor of Wymering and followed its descent.

The name-dropping does not quite end there, for we have another area to consider, the part we now know as East Cosham. Held by Maud de Bokland in the twelfth century, it was never called a manor, but was merely known as land in East Cosham. From Maud it passed into the hands of the Maundeville family for several generations, until William de Maundeville gave it to Geoffrey de Lucy, who sold it to Peter des Roches, the Bishop of Winchester. The Bishop assigned it in free alms towards the foundation of the abbey at Titchfield, and it remained under the jurisdiction of the abbey for many stormy years following, then after the dissolution of the monasteries the land at East Cosham was granted to Henry Wriothesley in 1607. At this point the record of the descent of East Cosham gets a trifle hazy, but by 1779 it was in the hands of Thomas Joliffe, and subsequently passed to Thomas Wrenford, Young Meller, and Thomas Gosling, who in 1821 sold it to Thomas Thistlethwayte, Lord of the Manor of Wymering.

So much for Cosham's early connections as a village. Just prior to the start of this century it was divided between two parishes,

"I remember it when it was just fields". Portsdown Hill from a rural Wymering.

London Road in quieter days.

8

that of Wymering, and Widley, but in 1894 they were amalgamated to form the Parish of Cosham.

As you may gather from the above, the history of Cosham cannot be told without the part that both Wymering and Widley have played being included. But, not wishing to blind our readers with names, we will skip as lightly as possible over the descendants of these two early parishes.

Firstly, we will deal with Wymering, referred to as Wimeringe in the twelfth century, as Wemering or Wymerynnge by the fourteenth, and gaining its present title by the fifteenth century. Wymering was possibly granted to the Albemarles before 1167 by the King, for at that date the Vidame of Picquigny, through his wife, held land there, she being the eldest daughter of Stephen the Second, Earl of Albemarle. The manor was held by William de Fortibus, the Earl of Albemarle in the reign of Henry the Third, and after he died in 1260, the manor reverted to the Crown. In 1280 it came into the hands of Eleanor, the mother of Edward the First, but not for long, for within a few years it belonged to John le Botiller by means of a part-exchange he made with his manor in Ringwood. Part of the exchange deal included a rent charge of fifteen shillings worth of corn that John had to provide for the master and brethren of the Domus Dei in Portsmouth.

John de Botiller died in 1309, and his descendants held Wymering until the end of that century, when it passed into the hands of the Wayte family, who held it for nearly two hundred years. By 1604 the manor was in the possession of the Bruning family, and as stated previously included the village of Cosham, but not East Cosham at that point of time. It is recorded that Thomas Gosling sold the manor to Thomas Thistlethwayte in 1821, and the Thistlethwayte family remained as Lords of the Manor of Wymering for a great number of years, lasting well into this century.

In the 1850s the parish of Wymering included the village of Wymering, half of Cosham village, part of the lofty range of Portsdown Hill and the hamlet of Potwell, plus the hamlet of Hilsea. To give readers an idea of the size of the parish, it comprised 3,545 acres of land which housed only 751 inhabitants, so as one may imagine, there were no problems regarding over-crowding!

And now for the parish of Widley connection, known as Wydelig in the twelfth century, as Wydele by the fourteenth, and by its present title in the sixteenth. The Earls of Albemarle held Widley as under-tenants in the 13th century, they were succeeded by the Scures family until 1428, when we find it is in the hands of the Uvedales. The manor remained in their possession for many years, in fact until 1618 when William Uvedale conveyed it to Sir Francis Neale and Edward Woodward, evidently for the purpose of a settlement. For the next couple of hundred years Widley had various names at its helm, including that of Brown, Griffith, Maidment and Woodrow, until the mid-1800s when it was held by the Thistlethwaytes of Wymering. At that time Widley parish included parts of Cosham village, also parts of Potwell and Purbrook hamlets. As stated previously, Widley parish was amalgamated with Wymering parish in 1894 to form the parish of Cosham. This made sense, for Cosham village had grown larger than its two neighbouring villages.

Cosham In The Middle Of The 19th Century

We have now reached the period when we can discard our doublet and hose, and pass on our armour to the nearest scrap-merchant, for we shall be having a look at the kind of scene that Cosham presented in the last century. Most towns or villages possess their "main drag", for Cosham this just has to be its High Street, and if we think that this street is busy with traffic now,

Rare print of Widley Windmill, depicting the building of Fort Widley in 1862. The Duke of Cambridge and his staff are inspecting the work.

Cosham High Street, 1905. Boxall's the ironmongers on the corner of Southampton Road.

imagine what it would be like without the by-pass roads and motorways that have been added within the past fifty years or so. Prior to this, Cosham High Street provided the main road route to London from Portsmouth, and during the halcyon days of coaching in the last century its cobbled surface rang to the sound of clattering horseshoes, the posthorn, and desperate cries from passengers who no doubt wished that they had not partaken of quite so much ale at the last coach stop!

Tales of the Portsmouth Road have filled many books, and it is understandable why Cosham has featured in these, by reason of its situation at the foot of Portsdown Hill, coachdrivers were either apprehensive at having to ascend the steep hill slopes after leaving the village, or delirious with relief at descending safely without their coach ending up in a ditch. Most of the towns and villages along this route to London geared themselves to the needs of the coach trade, with inns, taverns, and blacksmiths all making a good living. Cosham was no exception, hence the large number of refreshment establishments providing alcoholic delight, there being at least six inns or taverns in the High Street alone!

Apart from the presence of the stage-coaches, Cosham in the middle of the last century still managed to retain its rural village appearance, its main hub being the High Street with its assortment of bow-windowed shops. Surrounding this thoroughfare there was very little in the way of buildings, just a few large residences and small cottages, most of these clustered to the east of Havant Road in the area known as Crooked Cosham, later East Cosham.

It is hard to imagine now that most of the Cosham area once provided an idyllic landscape of golden corn basking in the rays of the sun, with working horses plodding steadily across the fields to perform the many chores associated with running a farm. The two names that were foremost in the farming community during the last century are that of Peel and Pittis: George Peel was the proprietor of Wymering Farm, and he is listed in the 1859 White's Directory as being the proud owner of a threshing machine; not far away was the farm run by George Pittis and his family, known as East Wymering Farm. The Pittis farmhouse residence was opposite Wymering church, and as one may imagine, going to church on Sunday through the fields was a delightful experience with this particular House of God overlooking this pleasant rural scene. During long sermons it is understandable that the flock sometimes dozed and let their minds wander; it is not so common for the vicar to follow suit, but this did in fact happen one day in Wymering Church when the parson, during his sermon, became engrossed in watching a female farm worker pick turnips in an adjacent field. Through the church windows he saw her lean forward at an alarming angle, suddenly she went too far and fell over, flat on her face. The preacher exclaimed loudly "There, I knew that would happen", right in the middle of his sermon; his words falling on the ears of a bewildered congregation!

Apart from the two farmers mentioned, the area boasted several others during that period, these included James Allen, Thomas Copsey, James Dunning, Henry Hill, William Martin, George and Henry Monk, all in Wymering parish, whilst in the Widley parish part of Cosham were Joseph Caile, Nehemiah Sharp, Henry Westbrook and Charles Henbest. The latter also giving valued service to the community through his mill, known simply as Widley Mill. Dealing with the same food source, nearby was Portsdown Mill, run by jolly farmer George Wakeford. When one thinks about it, Widley was a marvellous site for a windmill, and what a splendid addition to the landscape it must have made in those days.

We mentioned earlier that there were a number of larger residences dotted around the district, and some of these were very imposing buildings, indeed. We have insufficient space to

Early print of the May Queen ceremony at Wymering.

The splendour of Wymering Manor drawing room

delve too fully into their history, but the following will serve as a reminder of a few of the houses that graced the Cosham district in the last century.

East Cosham House was the residence of the Rev. Edward Phelps, who was Chaplain of Portsmouth Dockyard. There was also East Cosham Lodge and East Cosham Cottage, with Mr. Peter West residing in the lodge, and Admiral Sir Lucius Curtis in the cottage. The Admiral was very well known in freemason circles, and was in fact the Provincial Grand Master of Hampshire for many years. He came from good stock, his father being Admiral Sir Roger Curtis, who was created a baronet in 1794 for his gallant conduct as captain of Lord Howe's flagship whilst in battle. Sir Roger lived in Gatcombe House near Hilsea, until his death in 1816.

Cosham Lodge was the seat of John Burrill Esquire, who also had estates at Hilsea and Stubbington, and also owned several cottages around Cosham. The estate agents of today would certainly have used their "very desirable property" term in praise of East Court, a handsome mansion with beautiful grounds commanding extensive views over Portsmouth and Langstone Harbours, the proud owner in the 1850s being Captain Frederick Warren. Many Cosham people will have fond memories of this resplendent house in later years, and Mrs. Florence Gardner has more reason to remember it than most folk, for she spent her childhood at East Court in the early part of this century.

Born in 1899, Florence was one of the ten children of Alfred and Charlotte Tree, and somehow they all managed to live in the tiny lodge attached to East Court. Alfred was batman to Major Brightsmith in the Boer War, the major being the owner of East Court, and after the war he retained Alfred Tree as his gardener and groom. Eventually Major Brightsmith sold the big house to Colonel Gwatkin, but the Tree family stayed on, and Charlotte served the Colonel as a cook and housekeeper for many years.

Florence and her brothers and sisters helped their mother and father with the chores, such as dusting in the house, or working in the garden, but their favourite pastime was playing in the orchard. Also in the grounds was a lovely path known as Lover's Lane, edged with an unusual pale pink lily-of-the-valley.

At the age of seventy in 1969, Florence made a sentimental visit with her sister Ada and her brother John to the old house in Havant Road, this was just prior to its demolition. It provided a poignant moment as the trio stood looking at the big house and the little lodge, the memories of childhood flooding back. Soon East Court would be no more, the end was near for this mansion that had so often provided the venue for the meeting of the local hounds, the demolition hammer was about to fall. Thirteen years on, only Florence Gardner has those memories of East Court in its heyday, for she is the only surviving member of the large family reared by Alfred and Charlotte Tree.

Let us return to the last century, and take a look at some more of those fine old houses. Travelling in a westerly direction, we would have found Portsdown Lodge, another handsome mansion set in 37 acres of park and pleasure grounds with fine views over the harbour. This was the seat of Admiral Sir Francis Austen, a courageous old seadog who had a remarkable naval career that earnt him the many honours that he had bestowed on him. He was the brother of Jane Austen, the famous authoress.

Wymering House was the residence of John Martin, a very well known Portsmouth business man. One of John's great passions in life was literature, an interest he shared with his neighbour, Vicar Henville. Henville was a bachelor for most of his life, preferring the company of books to females, but to the amazement of his friends when he was at a very advanced state of life he married a pretty young thing. Unlike her husband, she was not a bookworm, and showed a liking for horseflesh, hence the fine team of horses kept in the stable behind the vicarage. Still with

War workers at Wymering Manor in 1916.

The resplendent Wymering Manor House.

gentlemen of the cloth, one of the most formidable names from the last century is that of Nugee. Wymering vicarage was consolidated with the rectory of Widley in the early 1800s, and the right of presentation to the consolidated benefice was bought from Thomas Thistlethwayte by Francis Nugee Esq., in 1847 for his family. The commodius rectory house was taken over by the Reverend Andrew Nugee, and, apart from his religious duties, he was largely responsible for the foundation of an education system in Cosham, about which more follows later.

Like most villages of that period, Cosham was very self sufficient, and its small shops and businesses endeavoured to cater for the needs of its residents. One of the most vital members of the commercial fraternity was the village blacksmith, and flexing his muscles under the spreading chestnut tree at the top of the High Street was Mighty Dick Boxall. Apart from shaping horseshoes, Dick had a rather unusual sideline, he was also a china dealer. But transport was the family's main business, and whilst Dick dealt with the horses, John Boxall was more concerned with what they pulled, he was a well known Cosham wheelwright. On the same theme, on arriving by rail in Cosham, if one wanted to hire a pony and trap to tour the district, the chap to see was William Blunden. As well as hiring out transport, Mr. Blunden was also the proprietor of a flourishing drapery establishment.

Whilst farming appeared to be the main industry in Cosham, another local enterprise was the manufacture of sieves and baskets, in fact, this was quite big business in the East Cosham area. The biggest basket establishment in the Cosham of the last century was that under the proprietorship of John Fullick, and in those days baskets were made to last, unlike the brown carrier bags that replaced them in later years.

Right, so now we have our basket, let us see about filling it with the food essentials of life. For our groceries there were the shops of John Allen, James George, John Jackson, John Lunn and John Windebank. For our daily bread we would also have visited the stores of Jackson, Lunn and Windebank, they were also bakers. Although many people lived off the produce from their gardens, and were by necessity vegetarians, those who could afford meat got their supplies from butchers such as William Davey or Henry Nargot.

Although we now imagine the old houses of days long gone to have huge log fires burning in the hearth, coal was a desirable commodity, and for this purpose there were a number of coal merchants in Cosham, names such as Earl, Grant and Wildey.

Many of the High Street stores specialised in one particular form of goods, but you will always get at least one individual who has aspirations to become Mr. Woolworth, and try to sell the lot. Such a chap was Thomas Baker, who had his finger in several pies. Thomas was the first chemist in Cosham, and we would guess that many readers will remember this family business next to the Swan Inn in the High Street, for it survived into the 1950s. Thomas Baker started his empire in 1845, his services including those of druggist, stationer, agent for the Royal Insurance Company, and postmaster. In the latter position, he was known by everybody in the Cosham district, and naturally, he knew everybody. In 1893 he gave up his postal duties, and the name on the shop fascia was changed to Baker & Son, giving Thomas a well-deserved rest. After this Mr. Hewlett was appointed post-master, he had four postmen attached to his office, and they were the first postal workers in Cosham to be kitted out in uniforms.

As well as basket making, another small industry in Cosham was thatching, and there were several examples of local workmanship scattered around the area, even in the late 1920s there still stood a thatched cottage on the corner of Havant Road and Court Lane, reputed to be 400 years old. It is rather amusing really, for houses with a thatched roof are now highly desirable and fetch a good price, and yet in olden times it was the peasants who lived in thatched buildings, the more wealthy folk living in houses that had slates on the roof. Anyway, one of the finest thatchers in the Cosham district lived in an old cottage at the bottom of Mulberry Lane, it had a thatched roof of course. This craftsman had an old fashioned recipe for curing rheumatism, it was reputed to have been handed down through generations of his family. What was the recipe? It was really very simple, when getting dressed in the morning, always put on your left stocking first!

Try to imagine the excitement when Cosham was lit by gas for the first time, this happened in 1875, with the gas being manufactured at the new works situated on a piece of land on Cosham Park. A short time prior to this a company had been established by Mr. John Douglas, who undertook to pay the proprietors a dividend of 6% on their capital. At the grand lighting-up ceremony, the first lamp was lit by the Mayor of Portsmouth, Mr. R. Davies, who was also a director of the new gas company. The ceremony over, and Cosham lit up externally, the group of dignitaries retired to the nearby Swan Inn to get lit up internally. Drainage was a regular case for complaint in the last century, and in the early 1800s a drainage scheme for Cosham was discussed, but the debates went on for several years, and the scheme was not passed until 1890. It was also decided in that year that the street lamps should be lit all the year round. We think it would be fair comment to say that when Portsmouth took over in the 1920s, Cosham enjoyed numerous improvements in its services.

We hope the preceding pages have given readers some degree of insight into what life was like in Cosham in the last century, and in the following pages we will be dealing more specifically with some of the places and events that have played a part in the history of the village.

Going To Church In Cosham

Looking at modern life, one is apt to think that it may revolve around such objects of adoration as the motor car, or that idiots' lantern that stands in the corner of our living rooms known as the television set. In years gone by, without the distraction of these objects, life revolved around the church. Sunday was the big day of the week, the day we downed our tools of labour, donned our best suits and dresses, and took our pew in the House of God. The churches were more than places of worship, they provided a meeting place where, after the service, the local folk could chat and find out what was happening in their community, or perhaps what was happening in the world outside. It is all too easy nowadays, all we have to do is flick a switch for "News at Ten".

Owing to its position on the main road to London, Cosham did not have the presence of as many churches, as it had public houses. The main place of worship, Wymering Church, could not exactly be described as being sited in a central position to the village, for as mentioned previously the parishioners had to make a trek through the fields to reach it on the western side of the district. Very pleasant in the summer but not so nice in the winter months.

The *Victoria History of Hampshire*, published in 1909, includes a very detailed description of Wymering Church in its section on the Portsdown Hundred, we do not intend to cover it as thoroughly in this small book, but will mention some general points of interest about the church.

The church of SS. Peter and Paul in Wymering, is a handsome Norman structure of flint with stone dressings, comprising a chancel, nave, aisles, north vestry, and a south porch. At the west end of the nave is a wooden bell turret with two bells, this replaced a small embattled west tower that was removed in 1860. The north arcade of the nave belongs to the latter part of the 12th

Wymering Church

Century, and is probably the oldest part of the church, the south arcade was added around 1220, and the chancel was probably rebuilt about the same time. The register dates from the 1600s.

Throughout its history Wymering Church has been subjected to several restorations, the most drastic taking place in 1860; there is no doubt that during this work it lost several historic pieces from its past. Whilst the restoration work was being carried out an interesting discovery was made, a tomb was found that was presumed to be that of the founder, but after investigation it was found to be too small for an adult. The theory was then offered that the chapel was founded by John de Wymering in memory of a deceased child. During the same restoration in 1860, a painting of Saint Christopher was found over the north arcade of the nave.

It was revealed in 1922 that Wymering Church desperately required more restoration work, but the big snag was lack of funds. The parishioners rallied round magnificently, and set about raising the money for the work. One of the local people who was in the forefront of the "Save Wymering Church" scheme was Mrs. Mulligan of Little Wymering Farm, one of her most successful ventures being a grand concert in the Albert Road Drill Hall, attended by the Mayor and Mayoress, Alderman and Mrs. Porter. It was an evening of mirth, melody and mystery, the latter being provided by Professor Reed-Ford with his magic act. Anyway, after a lot of hard work throughout the district, the money required was raised, and the work was carried out, much to the relief of the Rev. Edgar Babbage.

Whilst the Rev. Andrew Nugee played a prominent role in Cosham's spiritual and communal life, the vicar that most folk will remember is the Rev. Edgar Babbage, for he served Wymering from 1912, and he remained there for nearly forty years. He certainly set a record for service that would be hard for anyone following to emulate, one of those being the Rev. Harry Gilroy who took over Wymering Church in 1951.

To conclude our brief reminder of Wymering Church, it is interesting to note that the elementary school building in the High Street was also licensed for divine worship, a portion was screened off to serve as a chancel.

Another place of worship in the High Street was the old Faith Mission Hall, serving those of the Evangelical persuasion in the area. This was sited next to Whitmore Jones, the house furnishers on the same side as the gas showroom. Prior to the 1920s the Mission Hall was the first building you would have come to on that side of the road when walking up the High Street from the railway crossing, public tennis courts were on the land later taken over for shops and a cinema.

A chapel was erected for the Baptists in 1871 on the Havant Road, situated rather like a rose between two thorns, with a public house either side in the form of the East Cosham Tavern and Uncle Tom's Cabin. The church building has seen many alterations since its origination, but still stands in the same position, with one public house less to combat.

Not far away on the other side of the road to the Baptist Church, stands the Roman Catholic church, St. Colman's. This is a fine building of stone and flint with a square tower, built and dedicated in 1929. Prior to the building of this church, the Catholics had to travel to the Military Roman Catholic Church at Hilsea.

Also in the same area, nearby in Penrhyn Avenue the Church of the Resurrection was built in 1930, the cost of £10,000 coming from the Bishop of Portsmouth's Building Fund. Formed in the Gothic style and comprising a nave, north and south aisles, chancel and bell tower, the first services were conducted by the Rev. Leatherdale, the Rector of Farlington.

If we return to the High Street, and proceed down past the railway crossing, up Hawthorn Crescent we will find the Church of St. Philip, an ecclesiastical parish formed in 1937. And that really covers most of the places of worship close to the centre of Cosham, one has to draw a line somewhere. Needless to say, all the churches mentioned have provided good service through the years, catering for our various needs, whether it may be for birth, marriage or death. Whilst mentioning marriage, one Cosham lady who kept the parsons busy was Jane Whall, whose claim to fame was that she was married a total of seven times. Mind you, she was a trifle unlucky with husband number six, she found out too late that he was married already, and he spent the rest of his honeymoon in Winchester jail. Anyway, Jane appeared to thrive on her marriages, for she died at the ripe old age of 81 in 1929.

The churches of yesteryear appeared keen to adopt the policy of "Catch'em Young", for one of the great attractions for youngsters belonging to the Sunday Schools were the wonderful outings. We expect many readers will have fond memories of being jammed into a horse-brake or motor charabanc, and being whisked off to such exotic places as Bognor, Littlehampton or Lee-on-the-Solent. Childrens outings such as these are not very common today, the family motor car has opened up new worlds, and yet not so long ago a tramride over the hill was looked upon as a great adventure.

Although that finishes our look at orthodox churches, we must not forget the open-air churches in the street. One of the most popular places for those with varied religious beliefs to meet was at the top of the High Street in Cosham, near the old fountain. All kinds of strange-looking characters would take a stance at this spot, and start preaching to one and all about the virtues of their particular belief, human nature being what it is, in a very short while they had a crowd assembled about them.

The word of God even arrived on wheels to the village of Cosham, the Motor Mission Van being a regular visitor, and once again the corner of Havant Road and High Street was the favourite venue to stop and preach to anyone within earshot.

Pub Crawling in Old Cosham

As mentioned previously, Cosham had a rather abnormal number of inns and taverns compared to the average village, the reason being its position on the Portsmouth to London road. Through the years, unlike many towns and cities, Cosham has not witnessed the mass closure of its public houses, and is still endowed with a reasonable number of these places of alcoholic delight.

We will commence our pub crawl in the High Street, by the railway crossing, just a few short steps away we will find the welcome portals of the Railway Hotel. This name will be unfamiliar with younger readers, they will know it better as The Rocket, for some reason the name was changed in the 1960s. But whatever the sign outside says, most Coshamites still refer to it as the Railway Hotel. This inn is not as old as some of the other establishments, for as its name implies, it arrived with the railway era rather than the days of coaching, but nevertheless it has been in existence to serve glasses of good cheer for several generations of local folk. The name that most patrons will remember in association with the Railway Hotel is that of Florence Parsons, for this lady ran it for many years, originally taking over from Maurice Hunt in the 1930s.

Walking up the High Street on the same side, just before we reach the corner of Albert Road we would have found that very popular public house, the King and Queen, alas no longer with us. This hostelry dated way back into the last century, and the genial landlord in the 1850s was a gentleman named James Clarke. The King and Queen did not survive too many years into this century, and we would surmise that there are not many local people still around who can recall having a drink there.

On the other hand there must be a number of drinkers who can remember having a quick one in the Ship Inn on the other side of the road, for it only disappeared from the High Street within more recent years. If they used this pub in the 1920s, 30s and 40s, they were probably served by Charlie Privett, the popular landlord there during that period. Not very far away from the Ship Inn there was the Swan Hotel, which we are pleased to say is still on the corner of Wayte Street, or Southampton Road, as it was known previously. and still providing pints for pleasure.

Walking, or perhaps by now staggering, further up the High Street, just past the National School we would have found The Falcon, another public house now long gone. The Falcon was a relic from the days of coaching, and the sound of the posthorn to David Minchin, the proprietor, was like money rattling in the till.

Cosham High Street, showing the King & Queen on the right.

The Ship Inn.

It is understandable that when this pub closed in the 1920s it was not particularly missed, for there were so many others of its kind in the High Street, and one of these was the George and Dragon opposite. This also was once an old coaching inn, although it has had several alterations through the years, don't let the date 1887 under the top fascia mislead you. James Rogers was the familiar face behind the bar in the middle of the last century, but leaping on through the years, the proprietors' names that may strike a bell are those of Walt Reed and Jack Fuggle. At present, the site of the George and Dragon is in doubt.

As readers may have gathered by now, there were at least five taverns grouped in fairly close proximity to each other in the same street, and one may venture to guess as to how they all made a living, even with the passing trade in this main thoroughfare. There is not much doubt that Monday was the big day for trade, for this was market day, and local farmers herded their cattle into the compounds at the top of the High Street. The market still operated into the 1930s, then the Odeon Cinema was erected on the site. Anyway, when it was in its heyday the local pubs provided a favourite venue for the farmers to conduct their business, price haggling being on the menu.

One rather unusual fact regarding the pubs in Cosham, is that with the centre of the High Street acting as a boundary, one side of the street was in Wymering parish and the other was in Widley parish, this being the situation before the amalgamation of 1894. It was therefore, possible to stagger out of The Ship, The Swan or The Falcon, all in the parish of Wymering, into the King and Queen or the George and Dragon, both in the parish of Widley, just a short lurch away!

One of the most interesting public houses in Cosham just has to be the Red Lion, the old building of course, not the structure that we know today. The original was pulled down in 1928 for road widening purposes, this being for the introduction of the new spur road. The old Red Lion was erected around 1560, and over the following years the premises were enlarged and extended, chiefly by the demolition of a very old cottage that stood nearby. Stories abound about the old inn, and it would appear that its large cellars were used at various times for smuggling.

Around 1820 the village wheelwright, Rickard Buckingham, was the landlord of the Red Lion, and whilst he was in charge there was certainly no trouble with drunks, for Richard was also the village constable. The inn passed into the hands of Henry Whiting in 1852, and Harry, as he was known, was continually harassed by the authorities for the billeting of soldiers and their horses, the latter being on their way to Portsmouth to embark for the Crimea. Harry's main gripe was that the Government only paid him 4d. per man and horse, which included bed and breakfast! It is not surprising that Harry went back to his old trade of bricklaying. Henry Shepherd took over as landlord of the inn for the following twenty years, then it passed to William Allee who was there for 25 years. Unfortunately, Mr. Allee met a sad end, he was drowned in Farlington Reservoir.

The Red Lion was a favourite stopping place for the old stage coaches, providing a good opportunity to rest the horses before embarking on the long pull up Portsdown Hill. The inn was also used for holding inquests, the coroner paying a fee of 2/6d. to the landlord for the hire. This was good business for the landlord, for at such events the pub would be crowded with onlookers, who no doubt quenched their excitement with a tankard of ale!

Not far from this corner of High Street and Havant Road, there once flourished no fewer than three other pubs. This may start a few heads scratching, most readers will know of two, but the third pub is very seldom mentioned nowadays. All will be revealed but firstly let us get the other two out of the way, there are no prizes for guessing that they are The East Cosham Tavern and Uncle

The George & Dragon, High Street.

The start of London Road, the old Red Lion is on the left.

The Swan Inn, 1930s.

28

The Falcon, High Street.

the Havant Road, within ten minutes or so you will reach the hamlet of Drayton, and the welcoming entrance of The New Inn. This is a very old inn that has seen Drayton grow considerably in the last eighty years or so into the busy centre it is today.

For those who possess a good stout pair of legs, and a head for heights, the George Inn still languishes at the top of Portsdown Hill. This is another hostelry that has watched the world go by over a good number of years, from horse-coaches to electric trams, from trams to buses. Apart from the passing trade, this pub always enjoyed good business whenever Cosham Fair was held, with jolly Jack Tars endeavouring to get young ladies who they had picked up at the fairground tipsy.

The George Inn also enjoyed sporting connections with

Tom's Cabin. Both these houses of liquid refreshment sat either side of the Baptist Church as mentioned previously, this was until the early 1960s, when both structures were demolished and replaced by one that retained the title of Uncle Tom's Cabin, So, how about the third pub? This was in fact but a few short steps away, on the other side of the road in Widley Street, and the name you may have been trying to think of was The Pure Drop. When one thinks about it, what a marvellous name this was for a pub. Florence Gardner remembers it being kept by a Mrs. Banks, but some readers may recall that in later years the proprietor was George Bridger. Anyhow, The Pure Drop is no longer with us, and neither for that matter is Widley Street. It was rather a shame when this area was demolished, for it had an atmosphere all of its own, in many ways like another village.

If you have the energy, or the thirst, you may be inclined to wander further afield in the quest for a drink. Carrying on down

The Pure Drop pub in Widley Street, Cosham, 1905.

The East Cosham Tavern.

Uncle Tom's Cabin during demolition.

Cosham, the game in question being bowls. The Cosham Bowling Club was formed in 1878, the founder was Mr. Leader, the landlord of the George, who had a green constructed at the rear of the inn. It was therefore natural that the club held their annual dinners in this establishment, and these affairs were magnificent, with the dinner being preceded by a balloon ascent and followed by a grand firework display.

Older readers may recall a great character who used to live at the top of Portsdown in the 1920s. He was known as Old Ned, and even at the age of 90 he could be found on most days sitting outside the George. Ned lived in a cottage named "Cory Cliff" and was the sort of character that one could hardly forget, wearing a white smock, a broad brimmed hat, hobnail boots, and a clay pipe stuck in his jaws at most times. To anyone who lent an ear, Ned would relate the story of his life, and such was his memory he could recall the old Rocket stagecoach travelling back and forth over the hill. In later years he became great friends with Jim Goble, Jim being a famous transport pioneer in the area who drove the three-horse bus between Cosham and Waterlooville. One of old Ned's pet hates was seeing females exposing their legs in short skirts, he considered this highly indecent. He also thought the world of the 1920s was far too much rush and tear; these thoughts coming from a chap who once walked to London, because he thought that trains were too fast! We wonder what old Ned would have thought of the 1980s!

We are now back in Cosham village, and our pub crawl is coming to an end, we sincerely hope that you have managed to stand the pace. Most of the older public houses have been mentioned, but of course there have been a number of these establishments added in more modern times to cater for this expanding suburb of Portsmouth. To keep local publicans happy we will remind readers of The Salisbury in Lonsdale Avenue, The Manor House in Court Lane, the Ports Bridge Hotel in Portsmouth Road, and last but not least, the Wymering Arms for those in that part of Cosham. At this point of the book the authors would be obliged if readers would swallow the last dregs from their glasses as soon as possible, for we are now calling "Time, Gentlemen, Please".

The George Inn in tramway days.

Back To School

"Schooldays are the happiest days", so the saying goes. But are they? It could be that it was like being in the Army, on looking back one tends to only remember the good times and forget the times that the sergeant major had his charges doubling around the parade ground in full kit!

Another similarity that the days of youth and Service life share, is that when you are in, you wish you were out, and when you are out, you wish that you were back in! In our schooldays, oh, how we wished that we were older, we could then smoke fags to our heart's content, instead of indulging in sly drags behind the doors of that inner sanctum marked "Boys" on the outside. We would be able to go into a pub and order what we liked, instead of having to take crafty sips from Dad's glass when his back was turned! But now we are older, how we wish we could return to those balmy days of youth! For one thing, if we had known that the skinny little girl who shared our desk, complete with pigtails and more spots on her face than Uncle Fred's dalmation dog, would grow into a little smasher within a few years, we would have no doubt shared our last gobstopper with her!

Just as many ex-Servicemen will never forget their sergeant majors, it is also a fact that most people will not forget their old headmasters or headmistresses, especially when they were called out in front of the class for "six of the best"! But generally, we harbour fond memories of our schooldays, and of the dedicated folk who struggled to drum the three Rs into our young craniums.

Right, we are now ready to provide a brief reminder of schooling in Cosham of yesteryear, so put away that copy of *The Magnet* that you are hiding under the desk, and pay attention, for we shall be asking questions later!

It could be said that the chap who started it all was a gentleman named Benjamin Caesar, for he was the headmaster of Cosham's

The old High Street school, before demolition.

first National School, opened in 1849. The original building was a former blacksmith's shop, but the building that followed it is the one that most Cosham folk will remember, for it reigned in the High Street until more recent times, more or less opposite the George and Dragon. Mr. Caesar was in command of this old school for over thirty years, and it was a sad loss to the community when he died suddenly in 1881. Fortunately, his place was taken by another dedicated teacher who won the respect of all his pupils, this was Mr. Budgen. Whilst he kept control of the boys, the girls were looked after by Miss Naish in the small school building in Albert Road. Both schools appeared to change roles through the years, with the High Street building conducting mixed classes at one time. The Albert Road school catered mostly for infants, and

*Cosham Girls' School choir, who triumphed in the Petersfield Festival in
1912. Miss Naish is the headteacher.*

34

before it was built the little ones had to attend classes in a small building in Havant Road.

The name of Caesar will always be associated with early schooling in Cosham, for Benjamin's daughter, Ellen, gave forty years of her life to serve as a teacher in the infants school. Miss Caesar was educated herself at the St. Mary's Home in Wymering, this was at the rear of the parish church, and the Rev. Nugee figured prominently in its administration. She also attended Cosham Grammar School, which was known as St. Paul's School and was sited on the High Street spot later taken over by the Faith Mission. The playground was entered through a lychgate off the main street, the gate was used later for Wymering cemetery. The lessons were conducted by members of a Brotherhood in the 1860s to 70s. They lived in Wymering Manor House whilst training to take Holy Orders, and helped out with church services and school lessons.

Ellen Caesar retired in 1923 at the age of 68, and died two years later in 1925. Mr. Budgen also gave forty years service to education in Cosham, until his retirement in 1922. We expect many older Coshamites will recall their schooldays under Mr. Budgen and Miss Naish, and perhaps also remember the great excitement whenever Empire Day came around, creating a good deal of patriotic fervour in the schools. On these occasions flags and bunting would be trundled out of cupboards as if by magic, and pageants and historical plays would be enacted to depict how Britain was so great. Whatever happened to Empire Day? Whatever happened to the British Empire?

Way back into the last century, the arrival of May Day was always the cause of much festivity, and a large helping of fun for the local children. They would assemble at a prearranged point, then walk in procession up and down the High Street in Cosham carrying long poles with large garlands at the tops of them. As they marched, the children would chant "The First of May is Garland Day, Please to Remember the Garland". The annual crowning of the May Queen also attracted many onlookers, the ceremony usually taking place in the grounds of Wymering Manor House. From the beginning of this century the May Day pageants were carried out under the patronage of the Squire, Thomas Knowlys Parr, and for nearly forty years Wymering Manor was the scene of much gaiety, with countless garden parties. These events sometimes brought Royal visitors to Cosham, and on one occasion Thomas Parr entertained Queen Mary at Wymering. It was reported that the Queen was enchanted with the manor house, a building comprising a mixture of several periods, and was particularly impressed by the tall chimney breast that housed the fireplace of the panelled hall. Thomas Parr was a great Cosham character, and always one for grasping the opportunity to wave the British flag, so it was not surprising that when war broke out in 1914 he did his bit by becoming a special constable, to be found on most days controlling traffic on the busy junction of High Street and Southampton Road. Thomas died in 1938 at the age of 75, and the last May Queen ceremony held at Wymering Manor before he died was held in 1936.

But, we digress, back to the kiddie-widdies! Unlike the many distractions on offer to children in this modern age, pleasures in the old days were relatively simple, with the visit of a magic lantern show to Cosham being one of the highlights of the year, this usually taking place in the Baptist Church Hall in Havant Road. On occasion, a travelling circus would arrive in the area, attracting all the local kids to the High Street to watch the animals being paraded in procession enroute to a nearby field off this main thoroughfare.

We should not imagine that there are many local folk still around who could remember Queen Victoria's Diamond Jubilee celebrations in Cosham, but with the aid of our crystal ball we can reveal that the local children had a marvellous time, with the grounds of Cosham Park being thrown open by Colonel Hunt, and amusements provided that included greasy pole climbing, the prize being a leg of mutton attached to the top. Not that the children wanted any more to eat, for they had already been given a large dinner of roast beef, followed by plum pudding. Anyway, that wonderful day was brought to its conclusion when a huge bonfire was lit on the Portsdown slopes.

Moving on into the 1900s, boys and girls had the opportunity in their after school hours to join such worthwhile organisations as the Scouts and the Guides. Under the command of Miss Foord-Angelo their captain, the 1st Cosham Girl Guides were a particularly smart bunch of young ladies, parading under the title of "Lady Pink's Own"; in 1922 they had their own new flag consecrated at a special service at the Baptist Chapel. The flag was presented to them by Lady Pink, wife of Alderman Harold Pink.

Every Mum in the 20s and 30s had dreams that their beloved child might be a budding Jackie Coogan or Shirley Temple, thus prompting them to drag their infant phenomenons along to the Cosham School of Dance, run by Madame Wheddon and Miss Roath. If local folk had the stamina they might pay a visit to the Drayton Institute, where under the guise of a dancing spectacular they might witness 50 child performers all trying very hard to hit the right note, accompanied of course by the aforementioned Madame Wheddon on her mighty piano!

As we have stated previously, life appeared much simpler in those days, and perhaps youngsters were all the better for it. Anyhow, we hope that we have provided an insight as to what life was like for the children of Cosham in days gone by.

All The Fun Of The Fair

It may seem a trifle late at this stage, but there may be a number of readers who are scratching their heads as to why a story relating to Cosham should be referred to by the title as "Fairdays", so we will attempt to explain. To the people of Portsmouth and the general Solent area, for most of the year Cosham was thought of merely as a sleepy little village nestling on the lower slopes of Portsdown Hill, coming to life only at such times when the Portsdown Fair was held, when thousands of pleasure-seeking visitors would converge upon Cosham by road, rail and tram to swell its population several times over. To them, Cosham was Portsdown Fair, at least for a few days of the year.

So, how did Portsdown Fair originate? It was really a spin-off from the Free Mart Fair that was held in Portsmouth, so we have to commence with a short history of that particular fair. In 1193 Richard the First granted the borough a weekly market and an annual fair, the latter held from St. Peter's Day for a length of two weeks. The Free Mart Fair as it was called, was a colourful affair that attracted merchants from all over the country to Portsmouth, several dealers even travelled over from France for this annual event. For those with money in their purses there was a wide choice of goods: pottery from Staffordshire, cutlery from Sheffield, cloths from the West Country, ribbons from Coventry, and baskets from Normandy.

When the fair ended after the allotted two weeks, quite a large number of the dealers and showmen moved their goods to the slopes of Portsdown, where they carried on trading for a further three days. Business was generally brisk, for as well as the goods mentioned above being on sale, cheese was also a popular line that drew the customers from far and wide. We might also add that a good deal of horse trading took place throughout the duration of the fair. To give readers some measure of its popularity, the White's Directory of 1859 lists the fair at Portsdown as a great holiday festival that often attracted as many as 20,000 people. The fair usually began on 26 July each year, and it is understandable that this date brought mixed feelings for the

Anyone for a ride on the musical horses?

Portsdown Fair at Bank Holiday time.

Pickpockets usually had a bumper day, and the local police were kept busy. At one time a hut was installed at the top of the hill whilst the fair was in progress, this was used as a temporary jailhouse, but more rowdies and drunks were kept in it than crooks and thieves. The latter proved harder to catch, using the large crowds as a shield whilst employing such devious means as the famous "Three Card Trick" with which to part people from their money. One well dressed gent at the fair certainly had hands faster than the eye, he would sell small purses for one shilling, and as the crowd drew around him they would see him put half-a-crown into a purse. Then they would buy the purse thinking that they had got the one with the silver coin inside, but after they had moved away to open the purse and examine it closer, they would discover that there was only a penny inside. Eleven pence for a purse that was worth 3d. in those days was not a bad profit!

Fortune-tellers made enough money in a few days at residents of Cosham, many of the local gentry objecting to having their peace shattered, even if it did only last three days.

Their wishes brought fruition for a while, for when the hill forts were built in the 1860s, the fair proprietors lost their site. But in the following years several attempts were made to revive it, and at one time it was held in the grounds of Cosham Park, not far from the railway station. In the 1880s the fair gradually moved back to the Portsdown slopes, this was largely due to the influence of a Mr. Sparkes, who will be remembered as the proprietor of the popular tea gardens at Portsdown.

Portsdown Fair had an atmosphere all of its own, attracting all kinds of life's travellers to its grassy slopes, an assortment that could be described as the good, the bad, and the ugly. Unfortunately, as well as the merrymakers, the fair also drew its share of con-artistes who were out to make a quick buck!

All the fun of the Fair.

Portsdown to last them several months. They comprised gipsy ladies with dark flashing eyes who all appeared to use the surname of Lee. Whilst Mum was inside the caravan having her fortune laid out before her, there were plenty of amusements to keep the kids occupied, swings, roundabouts, whirligigs, coconut shies, Aunt Sallys, and of course our old friend, the cakewalk. There were also a number of circuses and small zoos in attendance, and of these Wombell's Menagerie always drew plenty of youngsters. Rare animals could be seen for the price of one penny, and at one fair Messrs. Gilbert and Atkins exhibited a Nilghau, which turned out to be a horned horse from Hindustan. They also had two lions on show, which were so tame that the keeper could put his head in their mouths.

There were also enough attractions at the fair to keep Dad happy as well, these usually coming in the form of alcohol. Hawkers strolled around the ground with kegs strapped to their shoulders, and from these they sold measures of gin, well, what they purported was gin anyway. If you drank enough of it, one could easily be led into believing that it actually was gin!

There always appeared to be plenty of Jolly Jack Tars at the fair, with giggling young ladies attached to the arms of their navy blue suits. Before long they would end up standing in front of the boxing booth, where, on an entrance platform, an assortment of gentlemen with flat noses and distorted ears would dance around in rather scruffy dressing gowns, on the backs of these garments there would be names such as "Cardiff Bill" or "British Jack". Colourful gents with straw hats on their heads, and cigars protruding from their mouths, would challenge anyone to try and go three rounds with one of the pugilistic characters jogging about behind their backs. The challenge would very often be taken up by one of our naval friends, either trying to impress the girl by his side, or full of the courage provided by the effects of the afore-mentioned gin! Anyhow, the booth pro would make it look good for a couple of rounds, then decide that he had taken enough blows to his hooter, and deliver a knockout punch to lay the sailor flat on his back. These fights rarely went the other way, and if they did, it usually turned out that the sailor was really the Naval Heavyweight Champion of the Middle East!

Through the years the fair at Portsdown expanded considerably, and its more rural atmosphere of the last century was gradually replaced in the early 1900s by pleasure rather than business, the selling of cheese and horses no longer proving to be an attraction. This was a shame in many ways, for Cosham when surrounded by fields and farms had a stronger rural compatibility with Portsdown Fair, a point highlighted by the fact that in earlier times the fair was not officially open until Farmer Pittis wielded his scythe in the cornfield to cut the first golden sheaf.

The fair gradually petered out, and apart from the occasional visit from one of these childhood pleasures of the past, the Portsdown slopes lead a fairly peaceful existence these days. But, we still have our memories, the vast crowds, the colourful characters, the swings and roundabouts, not forgetting the smell. Ah yes, fairs had a unique aroma all of their own, a mixture of steam and oil liberally smothered with cockles and jellied eels!

Ah, if we could only return to those halcyon days of youth, if you went to Portsdown Fair with a shilling in your pocket, you were in Seventh Heaven!

Boots and Bedpans

For generations past the streets of Cosham have had their fair share of military boots tramping over their surfaces, and countless village maidens have received broken hearts through encounters with men in khaki. Silly girls, if only they had listened to Mother!

But, even in the days before the British soldier adopted a

Main entrance of Alexandra Hospital.

uniform of khaki, the area surrounding Cosham proved to be a popular venue for the military to practise their war-games. Camps were set up on the Portsdown slopes, and before long the air was filled with the sound of bayonet striking bayonet, with rival regiments charging over the hill with fiendish glee.

The good people of Cosham observed the military skylarking with a certain degree of amusement, but this feeling very often changed to wonder whenever a troop review took place on Portsdown, for these could be splendid affairs indeed. One of the most memorable was presented in 1882, this was for the Easter Review, and no less a personage than the Prince of Wales himself travelled to Cosham to inspect the troops and witness the mock battle that was enacted during the event. The people of Cosham certainly rose to the occasion, two large arches were erected in the High Street and almost every house and shop had flags and bunting draped across their fascia. For years after the review parents would tell their children about the great day when King Edward VII as a prince came to Cosham, and how it was the grandest sight that the village had ever seen.

That military review in 1882 took place following a terrible Winter the year before. 1881 was renowned as the year of the "Great Snowstorm" and the villagers of Cosham spent most of the daylight hours with a shovel attempting to dig their way out. The local conditions had a decidedly Arctic flavour, and the military camped on the hill slopes experienced a particularly rough time. In fact, there was an incident in which a young soldier was found to be missing. The soldier, who had recently returned from India with his regiment, was found later frozen to death on the hillside. Following this the War Office issued a request that no soldier should be sent to such a bleak place as Portsdown after returning from a hot country.

Of course, soldiers in the old days did not enjoy the standards of pay received by the Services in recent times, but they had little doubt as to how they were going to spend the small amount they got weekly from the hands of the paymaster. Friday night was the night for Cosham fathers to lock up their daughters, and for taverns such as the George and Dragon and The Falcon to have their hands to the pumps. When they had enough ale in their stomachs, they had a tendency to get obstreperous, this resulting in frequent brawls with the local lads of the village. But it was all good fun really, usually ending with the combatants shaking hands, then bathing their black eyes and bloody noses in the nearby horsetrough!

The military presence in Cosham took on a more permanent status in 1904, this was when the hospital buildings on the lower slopes of the hill were erected, the foundation stone being laid by Queen Alexandra, which explains why it was known as the Alexandra Military Hospital. The hospital gave good service to the military for over twenty years, especially during the First World War in 1914, then by the late 1920s it was taken over for civilian purposes and the name changed to Queen Alexandra Hospital. The "Q.A." has been expanded considerably in more recent times, and now ranks as one of the finest hospitals in the South of England, equipped to cater for the increases of patients from inner Portsmouth now that the city's Royal Hospital has closed its doors.

Although men in khaki are no longer plentiful in the streets of Cosham, there is still a reminder of military might on the hills around the village, namely the string of forts that were erected as a chain of defence in the 1860s. Of these great stone fortresses, the closest in proximity to Cosham are Fort Southwick, Fort Widley and Fort Purbrook. The Palmerston forts on completion were deemed obsolete, and looked upon as a folly, but they came into their own in the Second World War and proved to be a useful asset. In fact they are still an asset to the community as a tourist attraction, Fort Widley in particular providing a wealth of historical interest.

Military camp on hill slopes.

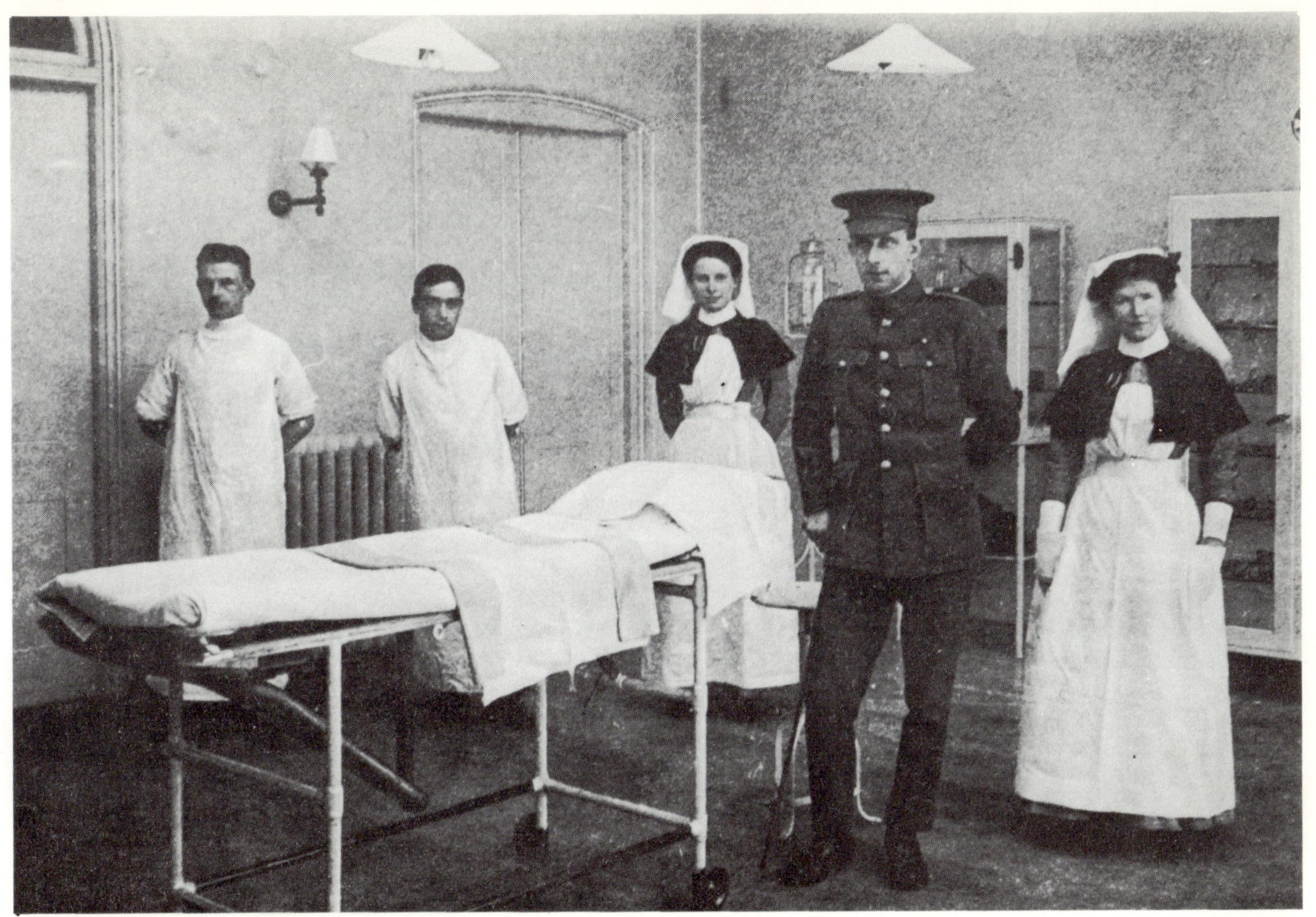

Alexandra Hospital operating theatre, pre-1914.

Alexandra staff and patients, 1916.

Making Tracks For Cosham

We have already mentioned Cosham's coaching days, and what a marvellous period that must have been, but one cannot halt progress, the faithful old horses were made redundant by the coming of the iron horse and the golden age of the steam train had arrived. We cannot pretend that Cosham railway station has a particularly colourful history, in fact happenings centred on the crossing gates appear to have created more interest in times gone by.

The White's Directory of 1859 proudly claims within its pages that the village of Cosham possessed a post office and a railway station, and indeed it had, the latter coming into operation when the rail link between Fareham and Cosham was completed in 1848 under the direction of the London and South Western Railway Company. The travellers of Portsmouth wishing to have an Away-Day in London had a choice of two routes at that period, they could make the journey via Brighton on the London and Brighton South Coast Railway, or travel on the westerly route via Eastleigh on the L.S.W.R. These routes were not very satisfactory, and most Portsmouth people plumped for crossing the harbour and catching the train from Gosport Station. This state of affairs was resolved later when the direct line to Portsmouth was opened via Guildford.

Unlike so many others of its kind, Cosham railway station has remained open and still serves commuters on the busy route between Portsmouth and stations in the western sector of the area.

One of the first chaps to wear a stationmaster's hat at Cosham station was Thomas White, and he and his staff did not have too many problems in the early days with the crossing gates, but towards the end of the century they were the source of hold-ups due to the increased traffic load on the road. Pedestrians also

Cosham railway crossing, Railway Hotel far left.

suffered the inconvenience of long waits at the gates in the years prior to 1890, leading to many heated verbal exchanges between road users and railway staff. In one of countless incidents at the gates, a well known Portsmouth clergyman got so fed up with waiting, he climbed the crossing gates. But he did not get very far, for a railway official appeared as if by magic and ordered the man of the cloth to return "from whence he cameth", and rather sheepishly the parson did as he was told!

Shortly after this the signal box was removed to the Wymering side of the road, and a footbridge was erected for pedestrians. We would hazard a guess that many motorists have a secret dread of stalling at a railway crossing on the middle of the line, or even of crashing through the gates, both incidents that Cosham crossing has experienced several times throughout its long existence. One

When the Railway Hotel overlooked fields.

Cosham crossing, note the trees instead of buildings further up the High Street.

that will be remembered by anyone who was in the vicinity at the time, took place in 1926. The gates had just closed, and the 8.52 from Totton was on its way, suddenly a car coming from the Portsmouth direction failed to stop and crashed through the gates, coming to a standstill in the middle of the line. Arthur Lake was the signalman in the box when the crash occurred, looking behind him, to his horror he saw the train approaching around the bend. Acting quickly Arthur switched the signal to danger and swung a red lamp outside his box, this was followed by the screech of brakes and sparks from the track. The train shuddered to a halt, just a few feet away from the car! Arthur Lake was rightly acclaimed to be the hero of the hour.

There was one crash at the crossing gates that has a humorous side. This concerned a character known throughout Portsmouth as "Dynamite Dan". Dan was something of an inventor, and his pride and joy was his very special bicycle, a machine that had sails attached to enable it to go faster with very little effort from the rider. "Dynamite Dan" was travelling on his sail-bike down Cosham High Street one day, when suddenly a strong gust of wind caught his sail to send Dan racing down the road like Flash Gordon! Unfortunately, the crossing gates were closed at the time! Crunch! Oh well, back to the drawing board!

As we stated previously, Cosham railway station is still in operation, and long may it continue. We will now briefly touch upon a form of transport that sadly is no longer with us, the dear old tramcar. Whenever old residents of Cosham are reminded of that wonderful transport system referred to as the Portsdown & Horndean Light Railway, you can be certain that a nostalgic sparkle will appear in their eyes, for the trams were once an important part in Cosham's everyday life.

Before the arrival of the electric trams, horse-buses operated from the Cosham railway gates out to Waterlooville, the end of the route being the Heroes of Waterloo public house, where the horses were stabled. In 1896 the service was extended as far as Horndean, but even so it could not by any means be described as a good service, and one could never be certain of reaching their destination on time.

Things could only get better, and they did, thanks to the influence of a renowned Portsmouth transport pioneer, Mr. A.W. White. This Captain of Industry was general manager of Portsmouth Street Tramways, and for many years he had harboured a notion to improve the transport system between Portsmouth and Horndean. The Hampshire Light Railway Company was formed in 1897, being a subsidiary of the Provincial Tramways Company along with the Portsmouth

Railway staff on Portscreek rail bridge.

Cosham railway station, 1904. When steam ruled the tracks.

Car No. 6 waiting at Cosham, 1903.

Tramways Company. When the Portsmouth Town Council took over all the tramways in the borough the Provincial Company was left with the tramway between Hilsea and Cosham, plus the horse-tram system over in Gosport.

A meeting was held at Cosham in 1898 with a view to running a light railway between Horndean and Cosham, and in due course the Commissioners granted permission. It was not all plain sailing, just one of the many problems being that Cosham High Street was too narrow for the trams, but this was overcome when the track was constructed on the west side of the village with a bridge to cross over the railway track. At one time because of objections from landowners it was thought that a tunnel would have to be built through the Portsdown Hill, but matters came to a happy agreement in the end, and the route went over the hill.

Work began in 1902, with the line being laid at the side of the main road for the six mile link to Horndean. An agreement was made between the Portsmouth Corporation and the Provincial to link the light railway with the Corporation tramways, the latter supplying the current to Provincial from their power station at Vivash Road. The two tramways met at a point south of Cosham railway gates.

The grand opening day arrived on March 2nd 1903, with the Corporation dignitaries accompanied by Mr. White travelling on the first car to Horndean and back. The run was proclaimed a great success, and a good deal of back-slapping was indulged in by one and all. Spirits were running high, no doubt helped by the free booze consumed at the opening celebrations, and many of the dignitaries voiced the opinion that this was just the beginning, it was Horndean today, and tomorrow the world! It was hoped that the line would eventually be extended out to Petersfield, and one can only surmise what a fantastic tramride this would have provided through the forests we now know as a country park, and over the majestic hills of Butser. There were also plans afoot to

Cosham tram terminal.

branch off from Waterlooville to Denmead and Hambledon, and to link Cosham to Fareham in the western section of the area. But, we are afraid the above dreams did not materialize, and the people of Cosham had to be satisfied with the track to Horndean.

The tramcars of the Portsdown and Horndean Light Railway certainly brightened up the local countryside with their presence, their livery of emerald green and cream providing a colourful addition to this historic highway. The service was regular, so travellers did not have to wait too long for the arrival of these iron monsters, in fact out of the fleet of 18 cars there were generally 10 in daily use. Even if intending passengers did by chance happen to just miss a tram, they could at least wait in the dry, for shelters were provided along the route, these were old tram bodies from the horse-tram days. The light railway company was rather astute

Tram No. 10 climbing the slope out of Cosham.

at utilizing obsolete equipment, they even used an old tramcar as an office at Cowplain, this being the famous LIFU steam tram that stood in the Park Lane depot. It had been hoped that the LIFU would one day revolutionize tram travel, but although this vehicle gave valuable service as a breakdown car, apart from some passenger use on the Guildhall and North End routes in the early days, it was only used as a workhorse whenever the electricity supply failed.

Prior to 1924, passengers wishing to complete the route from Horndean end through to Portsmouth had to change trams at Cosham, from P. & H.L.R. to Corporation, and vice-versa if they were travelling north. A permanent through service was agreed in 1924, thus allowing passengers to travel between the Guildhall and Horndean for 9d. Shortly after this, the line was extended in the south to Clarence Pier, so for the people living in the northern part of the area a day at the seaside was a relatively effortless journey, and the same could be said for the folk of Portsmouth and Southsea who wished to experience the delights of the countryside with a picnic at Portsdown or in Horndean Woods.

For tram passengers travelling from the Horndean direction towards Cosham, what a marvellous view they were afforded as they began the descent from the top of Portsdown, a virtually unspoilt and unrivalled panoramic view over Portsmouth to the Isle of Wight, so it was understandable that seats on the top deck were highly sought after, but only in good weather of course! One might also imagine that both tram crew and passengers required nerves of steel at times when making the descent down into Cosham, with these great lurching monsters being battered by gale force winds.

The part of the route at Portsdown was certainly interesting, as one may gather from the above, and tram riding also had its moments in the area south of Cosham village, where the

On top of Old Portsdown, one up and one down.

Passengers fighting for tram seats during Cosham Fair.

Prior to 1881 the Portsmouth Street Tramways were operating horse-buses through to Cosham, then in July of 1881 a system of horse-trams were introduced, terminating just beyond where the Portsbridge Hotel is now sited. The up and down tracks went separately through the two arches at Hilsea, crossing the swing bridge, there being two bridges across the moat at this section. Although by the end of 1901 electric trams were running in Portsmouth as far as Portsbridge, Cosham had to wait until 1903 until they could bid the old horse-trams farewell and gaze in wonder at the arrival of the new electric vehicles. As stated previously, the through link between the Corporation track and that of the Portsdown & Horndean system did not transpire until 1924, and it is interesting to note that in preparation for the link a sharp and dangerous bend dividing the two terminals was straightened out in 1922. So that this work could be carried out, an old wooden structure known by Cosham residents as the Black Hut had to be demolished first, but it only took place after a long wrangle with the occupier, who was eventually persuaded by the authorities to leave it for more suitable accommodation in one of the three council houses near the tramway terminus.

Going back to Hilsea, there is an interesting story regarding a tramstop known by local people as Copseys Siding. The trams were a popular form of transport with the military personnel of Hilsea Barracks, and so was this siding, for although the stop before it was the official one for the barracks, Copseys was nearer to them. This led to a number of arguments, for when the tram reached the official stage the conductor would call out "end of the penny fare", the general response to this was for the passengers to remain seated, they wanted to get off at the next stop but did not want to pay the extra 1d. to do so. The matter was resolved by a local farmer named Edward Copsey, he knew Mr. White the tramway boss, and wrote to him explaining the predicament of the passengers. Showing his usual good sense,

Corporation trams crossed from Portsea Island to the mainland at Hilsea. This was the spot known as the Hilsea Lines, fortifications of moats and drawbridges that were erected in 1861. For centuries the only entrance into Portsmouth by land was by a bridge spanning the creek at Hilsea, and for obvious reasons this was the prime spot for methods of defence.

The 1861 fortifications included a new gateway that was known as Hilsea Arches, a most pleasing structure built of red and yellow bricks, decorated in black bands with the letters V.R. set in the centre of the arches. The arches were negotiated fairly comfortably by the horse-buses and horse-trams, but when the taller electric trams were introduced one had the feeling that passengers on the top deck were in danger of having their blocks knocked off!

Hilsea Arches in horse-tram days.

Portsdown & Horndean Light Railway, opening day 1903.

Mr. White agreed to extend the penny stage to the siding stop, everyone was happy, and that really is how the stop became known as Copsey's Siding.

The Hilsea Lines area took on a new look in the 1920s, work on demolishing the arches and fortifications had begun in 1919, thus providing easier access for the trams. Another notable event took place in 1927, this was on 14 July when Mr. Frank Privett, the Mayor of Portsmouth, officially opened the new Portsbridge at Hilsea. The old bridge had become entirely inadequate for the increased flow of motor traffic by then using this only route in and out of Portsmouth, so the new bridge with a width of 80ft. was acknowledged by one and all as a vast improvement.

Meanwhile, on the northern tracks the resplendent green and cream tramcars of the P. & H.L.R. were still negotiating the ups and downs of the main highway between Cosham and Horndean.

The Fareham & Gosport Tramways system came to an end on the last day of 1929, being replaced by buses, and seven of its tramcars were transferred to the Cosham and Horndean service, thus increasing the fleet to 19 cars, after four older cars had been withdrawn from service. One interesting difference between the trams of the Portsmouth Corporation and the P. & H.L.R. was in the lighting headlamps, the latter concern having them fitted to the facia of the top deck, whilst the Corporation trams carried them on the lower portion.

But the end was drawing near for the Horndean trams, with motor buses and trolley-buses gaining popularity with their greater flexibility, the Light Railway Company agreed to cease tram services at the end of 1934. After the three months statutory notice had been completed this just took the service into 1935, when on 9 January the last green car left Cosham, a sad day indeed for tram-lovers.

The Southdown Motor Services was already running buses on the route to Horndean, and it took over completely when the last tramcar No. 6 had disappeared from view. Time was not wasted in removing the old tram tracks and standards, and within a matter of weeks there was not an overhead line or road rail to be seen along the whole route between Horndean and Cosham, a sure sign that buses had won the transport battle. Back to the area south of Cosham railway gates, the trams had already been replaced in the October of 1934 by Corporation buses, the turnaround point being at the Red Lion in Cosham. In the following year Cosham was to witness the arrival of that now revered form of transport known as the trolleybus, providing a silent service with the added bonus of being free from exhaust pollution. Why on earth did they stop using trolley-buses? Unfortunately, they did, and in 1958 Cosham folk saw the last trolleybus glide through their streets. The motor bus had gained another victory.

Demolishing Hilsea Arches in 1919.

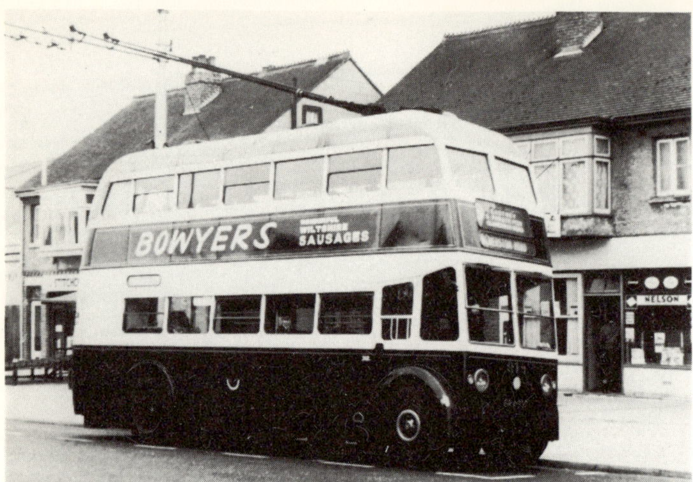

Trolley-bus in Spur Road.

 As this is not primarily a book about transport, we must now turn our minds to other things, but we hope that this brief reminder of Cosham's transports of the past has rekindled a few fond memories.

Leisure and Pleasure

Although folk in years gone by did not have the number of leisure hours enjoyed by their modern counterparts, they certainly endeavoured to get the most out of the hours that they did not have their noses to the grindstone, and we feel it would be true to say that people in earlier days had more of the community spirit.

In its village days Cosham had plenty of this community spirit, for apart from the activities for the youngsters that we have already mentioned, the adults were well catered for with several clubs and organisations on hand to keep local folk occupied. When there were more military stationed in the area, it was only natural that dances always proved to be a popular attraction for those who like to trip the light fantastic, and who could resist a soldier when he asked you to dance, providing you were a girl that is!

In those days we had not become slaves to the horseless carriage, taking delight in walking up to the top of Portsdown on summer evenings and Sunday afternoons. The tea gardens always did a good trade on the hill, older readers will remember Albert Sparkes as the proprietor, or perhaps Alf Hawkins in later years. For those who do not have a hankering for energetic sports, but still like plenty of fresh air, how about a game of open-air whist? Believe it or not, open-air whist drives were very popular in the Cosham of the 1920s, and at one drive in the gardens of Wymering Manor House over 150 players took part!

When Cosham was taken over by Portsmouth in 1920, its social facilities took a turn for the better. For those who like to curl up with a good book, their prayers were answered in 1924, when a branch library was opened in the High Street as part of the Portsmouth library service, then in the 1930s a more permanent library for Cosham readers was opened in the new Spur Road. Another advantage of being in such close proximity to Portsmouth was that when Hilsea Swimming Lido opened in 1935 many Cosham folk lived closer to the pool and pleasure gardens than most of Portsmouth's population, hence the endless procession of Cosham youngsters heading for Hilsea on fine days with towels rolled under their arms.

If you want to put your shirt on a horse today in Cosham, all you have to do is to stroll into the nearest betting office, but back

Wymering race-track, with Paulsgrove Halt rail stop at rear of stands.

in those balmy pre-war days one had the extra advantage of actually being able to see one's horses lose, more or less on one's own doorstep. We refer of course to Wymering race track, this may cause younger readers to look puzzled, for the site of the old race track has been covered with factories and housing for quite a number of years. But, it is true, there was a track just down the road by Paulsgrove, and like many race tracks around the country it also had its own special railway stop, this was known as Paulsgrove Halt.

Wymering racing track was opened on 10 August 1928 by promoter George Cooper, it was a 7½ furlong course turved from grass cut out of Portsdown Hill. Stables were available for 52 horses, and it had the usual stands, bars, cloakrooms, plus a car park for 2,000 cars, a sure sign that the motor car was beginning to make its presence felt. The opening programme took place over two days, and attracted over 125 entries. Whilst the meeting was voted a great success, the proprietor had a bit of bad luck in that when the track had only been open one week, one of the stands caught fire and burnt down, this was later described by onlookers as a blazing inferno. As if that was not enough, thieves broke into the race track offices the same week, but all they got away with was five shillings. Wymering Track also promoted the new sport of motor cycle racing, the first programme commencing on 25 August in that same year of 1928.

Although there was a number of local concert parties and drama groups in Cosham, the big attraction guaranteed to get residents away from their fireplaces was the lure of the cinema screen. Ah! those halcyon days of youth when we used to slip into the picture house through the rear toilet windows in order to spend a couple of hours with Charlie Chaplin or Shirley Temple. This particular subject has been covered to a fuller extent in another book of nostalgia in the Milestone "Down Memory Lane"

The Carlton Cinema, late 1930s.

series, namely *"The Cinemas of Portsmouth"*. But we will provide a brief reminder of some of our favourite picture palaces from the Cosham of yesteryear.

The oldest cinema in Cosham was simply known as the Cosham Picture House, it began life in 1921, and was sited between the George and Dragon and Woolworth's 3d. & 6d. stores. Built by Privett's, this cinema had a Tudor-style of architecture, and a first floor cafe that was aptly named "The Old Oak Tearooms". Although the Cosham Picture House dealt mostly in fun and laughter, it was the scene of a tragedy in 1926 with news that hit the headlines. This concerned the death of a young chap named Philip Marshall who was the projectionist of this cinema. He went down to the operations room to start the gas engine and unfortunately whilst he was bending over the machinery he became entangled in the fly-wheel and was mangled to death. But, the show must go on, and fortunately events such as this were not a regular feature at the Cosham Picture House. It was renamed in 1930 the Cosham Cinema, and a few years later in 1934 this was changed to The Waverley, a title that remained with this cinema until it was closed in 1939.

Luckily, Cosham still had two other cinemas, the first being the Carlton down near the railway crossing gates. This cinema was opened by Jack Buchanan in 1934, and at that time could be described as being one of the most luxurious cinemas in the Portsmouth area, even to the point of having an illuminated fountain splashing patrons as they entered. The Carlton had to close for a short while in 1940 when it was hit by an enemy bomb, but it was soon "business as usual". After the war it had a change of name to The Essoldo, and later still to The Classic, a name that still adorns the fascia, for this is now Cosham's only cinema.

Cosham's other cinema started life as The Ambassador, sited up the High Street on the old cattle market site. It was opened by Will Hay in 1937, and once again luxury was the order of the day, large entrance hall, sweeping staircases to an upper restaurant that had dancing facilities if required, just about everything including the kitchen sink. The Ambassador survived the war fairly well, and was given a new name in 1945, it now became the Odeon. Sadly, this cinema suffered the indignity in later years of so many of its kind, it became a bingo hall and social club. Still, we must be thankful that the building has not been demolished, and also be pleased that it still provides some form of pleasure. When one thinks back to the 1930s, it now seems amazing that a place as small as Cosham had not one, not two, but three cinemas all operating at the same time.

Good Morning, Can I Help You?

In all the "Down Memory Lane" publications it has become apparent that when dealing with a particular town or village, a large majority of readers have gone out of their way to express how much they enjoy being reminded of the old shops and businesses that flourished in their days of youth. We might add that whilst it gives pleasure to the reader, it can prove to be a headache for writers, for they never have enough space available to name every shopkeeper that existed throughout a period of more than ten years or so. However, in this section we shall attempt to please as many people as possible, and the period that we have selected covers the 1920s and 30s.

As far as Cosham is concerned this was a very important period, for it was expanding from a small country village on the London Road into a bustling suburb of Portsmouth. New areas of housing development were sprouting away from the High Street; to the west council estates erupted around Wymering and Paulsgrove, and in the east many private houses were built on both sides of the railway tracks. But not all the new developments in Cosham were welcome, many wanted the area to retain its village atmosphere, hence a petition raised in 1922 by the residents of Knowsley Road and Salisbury Road protesting about the new Eastern Road route that was extended through their roads. They stated that their once quiet roads had been turned into a main thoroughfare.

Older people are not always prepared to accept change, therefore imagine the feelings of old Coshamites when they saw so many things changing in and around their once country village home. These feelings were never stronger than in the 1930s, for they feared that Cosham might become an oil-town. This happened in 1936, when a 130ft. high derrick tower dominated the slopes of Portsdown Hill, and a hole was bored to unearth the

The Great Trundle. 1,700 mile walk by Hayes, Cosham High Street, July 16th 1907.

rich oil find that had been predicted by geological and mining experts. The drilling went on for a year and reached a depth of over 6,500 feet, and although some traces of the black gold were found, it was insufficient to justify further boring. The project was abandoned in February 1937, the hole was plugged, and the mining village that had risen around the derrick moved away in search of another find.

Although the rapid expansion of Cosham was not popular with all the residents, the local shopkeepers had no cause for complaint, business was on the up and the cash registers were clanging open and shut at a good pace. Although the High Street did not attract the attention of many large concerns, it had an abundance of interesting small shops that catered for most of the residents' needs; we hope that the following may jog a few memories.

Starting our stroll from the railway gates, on our right we pass the premises of coal merchants such as Colyer & Co., and Clements Brothers, the tobacconists shop of Frank Partoon, and even the Railway Hotel, for our reminder of Cosham shops really begins on the corner of Knowsley Road. This particular corner has housed a variety of businesses through the years. In the 20s and 30s it was the site for Arthur Wilson's boot shop, Rodolphe the mens outfitters, and for Street's Dairies. This corner now serves as premises for Shipp's fruit and veg. store.

In days gone by there was another fruiterer in the adjoining shop, older readers may remember Hanson's. Moving along we would have found the popular printing establishment of Mr. Bilboe, who operated from this High Street spot for many years. On the corner of Cosham Park Avenue was the premises of Tree Brothers, the well known ironmongers. In later years they moved further up the High Street to a site that is now occupied by the Midland Bank, in fact Tree Brothers moved their premises three times in all during their existence. This hardware business is well

remembered by Florence Gardner, who as Miss Tree served in the store of which her brothers were the proprietors. As with most trading establishments of this type, the pavement outside the shop was crammed with a variety of goods, from dustbins to watering cans. They all had to be put out in the morning, and they all had to be taken back in at closing time, a mammoth task indeed.

Moving over to the other corner of Cosham Park Road, in the late 20s we would have found Bill Coles' electrical shop, a sure sign that the new fangled marvel of electricity was beginning to make its presence felt. Next door was Alice Tucker's cafe, where both workers and shoppers could partake of a steaming cup of char. This cafe was taken over in later years by Jim Austen. The luxury of owning a washing machine was not within the reach of Mrs. Housewife in those days, so you can be sure that Chapman's Laundry office nearby was kept busy. Do you remember how they starched the separate collars we had in the old days, we used to finish the day with multi-coloured necks.

In this parade between Cosham Park Road and Magdala Road there were a number of businesses, names such as Dorothy Cooper's hat shop, Arthur Oldman the hairdresser, Smeed & Smeed the wine merchants, Madame Norreys the drapers, and George Beckett's tobacconists shop. Then on the corner of Magdala is an old established boot and shoe shop that we are pleased to say still has the same name on the fascia, the family concern of Arthur Christopher.

In the next block we are also delighted to note that another High Street name from Cosham's past is still flourishing in the fried fish business, the family name of May, starting with John in the late 20s, transferring later to Arthur. Not far away we had one of Portsmouth's famous grocery names, William Pink & Sons next to The Drake. What a marvellous mixture of aromas the Pink stores conjured up, it was something that we will never savour again in this pre-packaged world of today.

Tree Brothers hardware store, High Street, Cosham. 1920s.

When you could buy a rabbit for 10d. George Burges shop in the 1930s.

Many readers will be surprised to learn that Fodens the much-acclaimed steam wagon manufacturers once had a depot in this block before reaching Albert Road, although by the late 20s the site had been taken over by Dashwoods the Undertakers. On the other corner of Albert Road Mrs. Daysh had her grocery shop, later a site for Boots the cash chemists. Mrs. Daysh had quite a bit of competition, for next door to her she had one of the vast chain of grocery stores belonging to the Portsea Island Co-operative Society. Then nearby, next to Miss Fullick's fruit shop, was another old-established fishmongery business ran by George Burges. So much for fish, that other food commodity known as meat could be bought a few doors away at Frank Burt's butchers shop, next to the Cosham Picture House. Both these establishments were taken over by the expansion of Woolworth's Stores.

The George and Dragon is no longer providing pints of pleasure, but older readers may recall that in the rear yard behind this pub, Horace Woods the saddler carried out his business when horses were still a common sight on our streets. Then came the cattle market already mentioned earlier, and next door to this George Boxall ran a grocery store. Next came a block of shops that were demolished in later years, the site serving as a car park for some time, although a parade of shops has been erected there now, but in years gone by it housed the premises of Philip Kent the watch-maker, George Smee's corn store, Charlie Privett the butcher and fishmonger, Harry Bateman's newspaper shop, and butcher Henry Smith, later David Brooks and the Co-op. One name that we cannot possibly miss out on this parade is that of Tom Pilcher the blacksmith, for he operated from this site for nearly forty years. He first came to Cosham from Portsmouth in the late 1920s, an ideal time, for the cattle market was still flourishing and there was also quite a number of farms remaining in the surrounding area. Although there were another two blacksmiths working in Cosham in the 20s, they were rather old compared with Tom.

Havant Road corner before demolition. The old basketmaker's premises are on the extreme right.

Although he worked on at his trade for many years, with the increasing popularity of the motor car the end was only a matter of time, and Mr. Pilcher made his last horseshoe in 1966. A sad occasion really, for if you lose your village blacksmith, a revered part of village life has gone forever.

We have now reached the turning point at the top of the High Street, so if readers would kindly cross the road we will continue our stroll by returning towards Cosham railway gates. On this corner of High Street and Havant Road we had Bill Brown's barbers shop, and before readers start proclaiming that his shop was not on that site, we must explain that he moved later into his premises in Havant Road, which those requiring a "short, back and sides" will be more familiar with. We might add that a bit

Bill Brown's barbers shop, Havant Road. Now demolished.

The Drayton of yesterday. New Inn on left.

Drayton in quieter times, Post Office on left.

further along from Brown's new position in Havant Road, before reaching Uncle Tom's Cabin there was the famous old family business of Fullick's the basket makers. Folk came from far and wide to this establishment, and it was fairly certain that they would find what they were looking for, for the walls inside and outside were festooned with baskets. Tall reeds were kept in water at the rear of the premises, and these were used for making such items as lobster pots.

This is where we must be careful not to get carried away, for before long we will be in Drayton with our wandering, so it is back to the top of the High Street for us. Next to Bill Brown's barbers shop there was Clifton & Mabbs the house decorators, and going past Budd's Place we had Mr. Underwood's fruit and veg. shop, later taken over by Henry Norton. Then we reach that part which until recent times housed Palmer's Olde Sweet Shoppe and has been replaced by a modern shopfront. Before it was taken over by Mr. Palmer it was the tobacconists shop of Eden-Smith, where readers may have bought their first packet of Wild Woodbines. If we raise our eyes to the roof of this building, we will see a statue of a rather vicious looking bird, this is in fact a relic from the old Falcon pub that once stood nearby.

Unlike the other side, this side of Cosham High Street appears to have been subjected to more physical change, although if one looks above the modern glass fascia of the shop fronts, they might be able to recognise the occasional clue as to the style of building that graced the High Street in days gone by. Moving past the National Provincial Bank and the old Elementary School, we would have found Campions the bakers, and yet another cake shop run by two spinster ladies named the Misses Couzens. Next came the dairy shop of Alf Streton, later the Southsea Dairy Company, then Mrs. Harrison's drapery bazaar, Arthur Corpes the barber, Albert Walter's grocery shop, Timothy Whites, and right on the corner was the forge of Ed Bance the blacksmith. This corner site was taken over later by Lock's fruiterers, and is now used for the same purpose by Elmes.

We are now at the junction of Wayte Street, only in those days it was known as Southampton Road. We do not wish to wander too far away from the High Street, but nearby is a reminder relating to the name of Wayte, namely the old Cosham almshouses. They were erected through the kindness of Honor Wayte in the year 1600 as dwelling houses for the use of four poor honest women on their own, and were rebuilt by subscription in 1818. Before we leave this spot in Southampton Road, some readers may recall that the original Post Office was sited just inside this road at one time, moving later to the other side of Northern Road.

Thomas Baker's chemists shop. He was Cosham's first postmaster.

The former Post Office in Southampton Road, opposite the present Post Office.

Havant Road Garage, Drayton.

Meanwhile, back in the High Street we will walk past the Swan Inn and Bakers the chemists, which we mentioned in earlier paragraphs, then in a parade that has now been replaced by modern buildings we would have found the premises of George Curtis the seed merchant, The Ship Inn, the surgery of Doctor Morgan next to the old Fire Station, Albert Ford's piano business, and, if we were lucky enough to master one of these musical monsters we could have had piano lessons from Miss Hudson next door.

Then came the Faith Mission Hall, which in the 1920s was the last building to be found before the railway gates, although in the developing years of the 30s several other establishments entered on to the High Street scene, Miss Morse's hat shop for ladies of taste, Whitmore Jones the house furnishers, the City of Portsmouth Electricity showroom and depot, Smith & Vosper the bakers, Butchers tobacco shop, and of course the Carlton Cinema already mentioned.

So here we are, at the railway crossing gates. Exhausted? We certainly are! Still, we hope that we have stirred a few memories, and if we have caused any reader to exclaim: "Ah, yes, I remember them", then we shall be happy. We warned at the beginning of this section that we did not expect to please everybody, but we humbly submit that we have touched upon over sixty Cosham shopkeepers from the past, and that can't be bad!

And so we bring our tale of "Fairdays and Tramdays", the story of Cosham, to a close. It is by no means the full story, but nevertheless it contains more than has ever been written on this area before, and as with all "Down Memory Lane" publications, we trust that we have provided good value for money, and above all, enjoyment for the reader. Happy Memories!

The King & Queen, High Street, when beer was a penny a pint.

GARLANDS
Booksellers & Stationers
115 High Street, Cosham, Portsmouth
(adjacent to level crossing)
Tel: Cosham 375633
Large stocks of pens from Parker, Sheaffer and all leading manufacturers.
Travel Books, Maps, Paperback and General Books.
Greetings Cards and Gift Stationery.
Open 8.30am — 6pm. 6 days a week